Self-evident
Solutions
for America

Stephen Arthur Murphy

ACKNOWLEDGEMENT

I wish to acknowledge the internet sites and news organizations where I gleaned many of the facts and statistics for this book. It is my hope that my readers will continue their interest in how our society progresses with fiscal responsibility and compassionate action.

CONTENTS

CONTENTS

PREFACE

We are Americans: citizens of the United States of America, a democratic republic of the people, by the people and for the people. However our nation has drifted from the founding ideals of "E Pluribus Unum" – out of many, One. For example, more than 90% of the growth in U.S. wealth since 1983 has gone to the top 10%: the bottom 60% has lost wealth!

In 2010, 46.2 million Americans lived below the poverty line and are the most since 1959. Many Americans are striving to make ends meet and feed their families. This is not sustainable because many see this as unfair and want to close the gap between the wealthy and the balance of Americans. Our nation was founded on these ideals:

The Declaration of Independence:

"We hold these truths to be self-evident that all men are created equal, that they are endowed by their Creator with certain unalienable Rights, that among these are Life, Liberty and the pursuit of Happiness. That to secure these rights, Governments are instituted among Men, deriving their just powers from the consent of the governed. That whenever any Form of Government becomes destructive of these ends, it is the Right of the People to alter or to abolish it, and to institute new Government, laying its foundation on such principles and organizing its powers in such form, as to them shall seem most likely to effect their Safety and Happiness. Prudence, indeed, will dictate that Governments long established should not be changed for light and transient causes; and accordingly all experience hath shewn, that mankind are more disposed to suffer, while evils are sufferable, than to right themselves by abolishing the forms to which they are accustomed. But when a long train of abuses and usurpations, pursuing invariably the same

Object evinces a design to reduce them under absolute Despotism, it is their right, it is their duty, to throw off such Government, and to provide new Guards for their future security. Such has been the patient sufferance of these Colonies; and such is now the necessity which constrains them to alter their former Systems of Government. The history of the present King of Great Britain is a history of repeated injuries and usurpations, all having in direct object the establishment of an absolute Tyranny over these States. To prove this, let Facts be submitted to a candid world."

The preamble to
The Constitution of the United States:

"**We the People** of the United States, in Order to form a more perfect Union, establish Justice, insure domestic Tranquility, provide for the common defence, promote the general Welfare, and secure the Blessings of Liberty to ourselves and our Posterity, do ordain and establish this Constitution for the United States of America. When in the Course of human events, it becomes necessary for one people to dissolve the political bands which have connected them with another, and to assume among the powers of the earth, the separate and equal station to which the Laws of Nature and of Nature's God entitle them, a decent respect to the opinions of mankind requires that they should declare the causes which impel them to the separation."

Abraham Lincoln's Gettysburg Address adds to the foundational ideals:

"Four score and seven years ago our fathers brought forth on this continent, a new nation, conceived in Liberty, and dedicated to the proposition that all men are created equal . . . that this nation, under God, shall have a new birth of freedom, and that government of the people, by the people, for the people, shall not perish from the earth."

What happened?

The word unalienable is now inalienable and means; not capable of being repudiated, absolute, and inherent. So we all have these rights given by our Creator and we should all enjoy Life, Liberty and the pursuit of Happiness together. Many of us clearly see this self-evident truth: the consent of the governed has been subordinated to special interests and greed. Instead of us all sharing in the blessings of this beautiful land, many corporations, politicians, wealthy individuals and institutions have usurped many rights of the people. And the gap between the wealthy and the rest of Americans continues to widen more rapidly.

Many Americans are now feeling and seeing the slow destruction of our nation of: We the People, and we are ready to stand united and call for changes to the very values and principles in which this glorious Union was born over two hundred years ago. We want to be part of the solution to bring fairness and compassion into every decision, action, and law.

We now live in a society where the pursuit of happiness is not the prime directive, but thoughts, words, and actions centered on "Me" are the focus of much of what occurs around us. What happened to all of us sharing the blessings of our wonderful Earth?

Joseph Campbell wrote in his book *The Power of Myth*: "The crucial question: With what society, what social group, do you identify with? Is it going to be with all the people of the planet, or is it going to be with your own particular in-group? This is the question that was in the minds of the founders of our nation when the people of the thirteen colonies began thinking of themselves as one nation, yet without losing consideration for the special interests of each of the several states."

Let us examine what "self-evident" means: evident by itself without proof or demonstration. Synonyms: obvious, self-explanatory. So something which is self-evident, many of us should understand. For instance freedom is a basic tenant of our democratic society set forth by our founding fathers.

The last line of the Declaration of Independence: "To prove this, let facts be submitted to a candid world." This speaks to transparency and honesty. It is a self-evident truth: many of our politicians have subordinated our rights to their own self-interests, such as re-election, personal power, financial gain, and a hefty pension. The Declaration states: "That to secure these rights, Governments are instituted among Men, deriving their just powers from the consent of the governed." Today, many Americans are dismayed by the lack of caring and sharing in our society. We will examine the facts and ponder possible self-evident solutions to help achieve our rights.

Our basic rights are defined as: a more perfect union, justice, tranquility, general welfare, blessings of liberty. These rights are spread unevenly throughout our society with the wealthy power brokers having them all, but not the rest of Americans. We all should share in the abundance described in the Constitution: ". . . among the powers of the earth, the separate and equal station to which the Laws of Nature and of Nature's God entitle them, a decent respect to the opinions of mankind." Notice the self-evident truth of equality stands pure and true in these wonderful words written over two hundred years ago.

We the people need to reexamine these facts and provide a forum for creating solutions for these all important issues, to ensure we rectify the inequality so we can truly have a society of the people and by the people that will not perish, but flourish and prosper.

When we stand together as equals, and bring forth our compassion, unity, honesty, and integrity, we will arrive at solutions which will help narrow the gap between the wealthy and everyone else. We need leaders who will be of service to these ideals. When all of us have the basic needs to be able to enjoy life; such as food, clothing, shelter, security, gainful employment, access to top-notch health-care, etc., then the pursuit of happiness can be truly achieved by all of us, if we intend for it to be so.

We Americans must desire to achieve these rights and make them happen. By honestly and sincerely working together to solve the many issues which cause the inequality we experience, when we look at the people around us as our brothers and sisters whom we appreciate and care for, will we truly arrive at sharing the abundance and living in peace and harmony. We are all part of the global community and when we act in accordance to the self-evident rights of freedom, equality, and happiness, these tenants of democracy will be evident all over this beautiful land.

A fact mentioned earlier is the widening gap between the wealthy and the rest of us. How do we solve this? Some of the self-evident solutions are right in front of us and we just need to articulate them succinctly and then work towards solutions. Some are simple and some are more complex but nothing is impossible when we all put our best efforts into unity and compassion.

Some things need to change. Change is a constant and we Americans must lead change where we want it to go, for the good of all of us. For instance when we think someone else or the government owes us something; we should look at all sides of the situation. Have we done our share of working to solve our own situations without placing blame elsewhere? This can be viewed as the "victim mentality" - when we don't hold ourselves accountable for our lot in life. Another example is when we have worked hard for our money or our place in society and we don't want to share some with others less fortunate. This is why we hear "mine" or "my" or "me" so often. What about Us?

We all live on this beautiful planet together and we are meant to share the abundance. This doesn't mean that those who work hard and set goals and achieve success can't still do that. Being industrious and successful helps others because this creates jobs and provides for much of what we hold dear. However gathering and hoarding too much is not the way to "share the wealth." Many of us have heard the adage, "We can't take it with us." Each of us should sacrifice some of our abundance to support our future and we should find ways to help those who are now less fortunate. We need leadership that is willing to tackle the tough issues and to teach, train, and legislate for the benefit of all Americans.

1 INCOME & WEALTH INEQUALITY

It is self-evident that if one person lives in a large house full of stuff and another is homeless and sleeping in a box under a bridge – many things are out of whack. For over ten years, the number of poor Americans has been rising. The poor consist mostly of the elderly, single mothers, low-wage earners, immigrants, the mentally ill, undereducated Americans, former inmates and now the shrinking middle class. Median household income in 2010 fell to nearly 1970 levels.

The poverty line is now set a $22,314 in annual income for a family of four. In 2010, 46.2 million Americans lived below this poverty line and are the most since 1959.

Today's poverty rate of 15.1 percent, matches brief peaks after recent recessions.

The top 1% of American earners whose real after-tax income has almost quadrupled in the past three decades, vs. about a 40% gain for the middle class. Let's compare the share of income by quintile. The bottom 20% of earners (income up to $16,358) have 4% of the income. The second quintile (income of $16,359 to $32,188) has 8%. The third quintile (income of $32,189 to $57,189 has 13% of the income. The fourth quintile (income of $57,213 to $97,298) has their respective 20% of the income. The top earners (income above $97,298) have a whopping 55% of the income – more than half of the country's total income. And the top .01% of Americans (billionaires) have 8% of the income!

The wealth gap has widened. Looking at wealth instead of income, the class difference is even more dramatic. More than 90% of the growth in U.S. wealth since 1983 has gone to the top 10%: the bottom 60% has lost wealth! While the sharp rise in unemployment has driven many families below the poverty line, this poverty rate has mainly been on the rise since the beginning of the new millennium. Many American families simply don't have the ability to make ends meet. Two of the reasons the poverty rate has increased dramatically is because of the reduction of decent-paying manufacturing jobs and the dramatic decline in housing values.

An interesting statistic and solution to reducing poverty in America: Social Security dropped the poverty rate from 22% to 11% from the late fifties to the mid-seventies. Social Security lifts many destitute elderly Americans above the poverty line.

During 2010, the earned income tax credit raised five and a half million people out of poverty.

Another solution has been the nonprofit Job Opportunities Task Force, where employers provide on-the-job training. This helps cash strapped Americans by saving them the normal up-front costs for job education.

Other possible solutions to lowering poverty are opening more accessible health clinics and reworking college financial aid so people could enroll in one class a semester. Also if we extended the earned income tax credit to all low wage earners, not just those who have children, this would help many Americans rise above the poverty level.

When we try to maintain balance in our society, one area stands out as unbalanced and that is the pay some receive for the job they do. One of the most important jobs in our country is the teachers who instruct our children, however their pay is not commensurate with the importance of their contribution to our society. Excellent education is tantamount to the success of America. A solution is to figure out how to reward excellence in teaching, so every teacher could aspire to greatness. Testing is one measure but others must be added to the mix to help ensure the teachers are not teaching to only raise their student's scores. Direct observation from senior teachers or others could be a way to add insight into the methods of superior achievement. Another possibility is to create a teacher survey filled out by their students and/or the parents. This process would not indicate who the student was but provide great feedback for improvement and for rewards.

On the other hand we have CEO's, investment bankers, sports figures, etc. whose income is exorbitant. We Americans need to insist on fair pay for the job done and tie that pay to performance. We have corporations, who by contract, reward their CEO's handsomely without regard to the whether the company is actually doing well. Stockholders should not allow this to happen.

This spread between those at the high end of the spectrum continues to grow between those who provide valuable assistance to keeping our country safe: police, fire-fighters, teachers, professors, etc. We should work together to close this gap and bring down the ceiling for the upper end so we can spread some of this income to those who deserve more.

2 TAXES

The tax structure in the United States is too cumbersome and it invites inequity by all the loopholes and ways for those who have the means to circumvent paying their fair share. We should streamline our tax code dramatically so transparency becomes the rule. Let us examine the tax rates for a "head of household." On the left are the current rates and on the right could be the new rates:

$0	to $ 11,950	= 10%	5%
$ 11,951	to $ 45,550	= 15%	10%
$ 45,551	to $117,650	= 25%	15%
$117,561	to $190,550	= 28%	20%
$190,551	to $373,650	= 33%	30%
$373,651	to $999,999	= 35%	35%
Above $1,000,000		= 35%	39.6%

This would shift more of the tax burden onto the wealthy and allow more money for more of Americans to spend on the basic necessities.

The next inequity which may be necessary is to eliminate all deductions, except for charitable contributions. This way someone making $500,000 would pay $175,000 in income tax and keep $325,000. An American making $50,000 would pay $7,500 in taxes and keep $42,500. Transparency would be a given because all people making the same amount would pay the same tax, unless they donated to charity. This eliminates the possibility for someone paying much less because of loopholes etc. Simple, clean, and fair.

Warren Buffett, who is one of the wealthiest people in the world, stated he has a lower tax rate than many of the people who work for him, because of tax shelters and loopholes. Warren's "Buffett Rule," is making the "effective rate" of those with income over one million dollars – 30%. Also Warren states that the bulk of income for wealthy individuals comes from capital gains and dividends. Capital gains are taxed at only 15%, but we could raise this rate to 20% or higher to bring in more revenue.

If we streamlined the tax code from the behemoth it is, to a few pages understood by all, we would be able to save tax dollars which are now going to the IRS and to many accountants for scrutiny of our tax returns. Possibly if someone only has income from a job, a tax return might not be necessary, because the tax would be withheld and sent directly to the IRS. Of course these proposed solutions would need to withstand projections to ensure the government would be able to operate with enough revenue to run a balanced budget and to reduce and eliminate the deficit.

There is a group of two dozen millionaires who call themselves, "Patriotic Millionaires for Fiscal Strength" and they have lobbied Congress to raise the tax rates for those making over one million dollars a year – to return to the rates before the Bush tax cuts (39.6%). They state that the gap between the wealthy and the rest of us Americans is getting to the breaking point, similar to where our country was just prior to the stock market crash and the Great Depression. None of us Americans want to go there and experience this, when we can show leadership and make the tough decisions right now.

Sales or use taxes hurt those Americans who have lower incomes because the percent of tax paid to income is higher for low income individuals compared to high income individuals. Sales taxes should be only levied or raised with fairness in mind.

Corporate tax rates are touted by some to be too high in America at 39% which is the highest corporate rate in the world. However with tax loopholes etc., this effective rate is more like 12%. For example, Exxon Mobil has been paying 18% and in 2012 this huge oil company earned $41 billion! The countries with the highest corporate tax rates are: America, France, Japan, and Germany. In Germany they have lowered the tax rate from 39% to 30% in the last ten years, but that 30% is the effective rate. On the other hand, three countries with the lowest corporate tax rates are: Ireland, Iceland, and Greece – and those economies have suffered financial disasters.

Another example of how corporations use loopholes to dodge taxes: setting up subsidiaries out of the country in a tax haven such as Grand Cayman, so the corporation doesn't have to pay tax on income generated there. Apple, Google and other tech companies transfer their patents to these subsidiaries so the profit from these patents evades US taxes. Another way these companies evade paying their fair share of taxes is to have a subsidiary in a state such as Nevada or Florida, which doesn't have a state income tax. Apple has a small office in Nevada and they funnel billions of dollars through this office to keep from paying California state taxes – even though Apple is based in Cupertino, CA. This is not fair to California, because many of the offices and employees of Apple benefit from California provided services.

These tech companies take advantage of tax loopholes over other companies which manufacture or sell products within the US. Last year, Apple paid 9.8% taxes while Wal-Mart paid 24%. As you can see, these huge corporations pay much less than many of us Americans – which is not fair.

We Americans should raise the <u>effective</u> corporate tax rate by eliminating many of the loopholes and simultaneously following Germany's lead in lowering the corporate tax rate to 30%.

Another situation to consider: the development of wealth and then passing it on to heirs. This creates inequality at the moment of birth, because while one person is born with the "silver spoon in his/her mouth," another is born into poverty. An increase in estate taxes would help here. Again, someone who has the desire and fortitude to forge ahead with their ideas and dreams, and make it happen, then hurrah for them! But when we pass on large sums of money or property to our children, we start the spiral of inequality even before they know any different. Some of this money that now goes to the "fortunate son or daughter" could be used to help the less fortunate – in other words, sharing the wealth.

As examples, Bill Gates and Warren Buffet, two of the world's wealthiest people, have decided to donate most of their immense wealth to help many of those in need.

3 RETIREMENT SOLUTIONS

Public sector pension woes are caused by ever more retirees' living longer lives, receiving ever growing checks from underfunded accounts. An example: lawmakers risked their political lives to put the Rhode Island retirement system on solid footing by raising the retirement age, tying pension increases to the health of the fund, and partially replacing guaranteed benefits with similar accounts similar to the 401(k). This is about the facts and the math, not politics, because the numbers don't lie. Government has obligations to the future as well as to the past.

The story of steadily expanding benefits with no corresponding increase in funding caused many to look at the facts. In 1960, for example, when the average life expectancy was about 70, a Rhode Island public employee could retire at age 60 with a pension equal to about half of his/her working salary – with no cost of living adjustment. However by 1990, life spans were five years longer, yet the retirement age had dropped to 50. The maximum initial pension had jumped to 80% of salary, and retirees were guaranteed an annual raise. With math like this, retiring from a government job in Rhode Island quickly became more lucrative than working at one. So, retired public employees could routinely earn retirement benefits that exceed 100% of their final average earnings.

A two-pronged solution: a diminished guaranteed pension together with a defined contribution plan similar to a 401(k), and this would apply to current retirees, not just future ones. This is fair and responsible and the notion of the failure to act is not an option.

Another comparison is the difference between Germany and Greece. During the 90's the German people worked hard and didn't raise their standard of living while much of the world prospered and grew more in debt with much of what seemed like free money from second mortgages etc. The

German people forged ahead and built a very strong manufacturing base which serves them well today. The retirement age in Germany is 67.

In contrast, many workers in Greece had government jobs which guaranteed certain benefits and the retirement age up to a couple of years ago was 50. As we know, the economy in Greece is close to collapse and only will survive with bailout loans from the European Union and the IMF. We Americans should take notice and learn from our global friends.

4 GOVERNMENT

The system of lobbyist's influencing some in Congress by financing their campaigns, and expecting something in return is not in the best interests of all Americans. Campaign finance reform is important so all contributions are above board and transparent for us all to see. Today, someone or some entity can donate large sums of money without the public knowing who or what is donating these funds. These "Super-Pac's" are now funneling millions of dollars into advertising for their candidate, and much of this campaigning is negative. We should set limits for political donations so one person or entity couldn't assert excess influence on a politician. It would be better for the candidates to talk about the solutions they have for solving many of America's issues, instead of berating their opponents.

Secrecy is another issue which clouds the truth behind campaign contributions. A self-evident solution is we should demand transparency for all contributions, so it is a public record who or what company or organization is donating how much to every candidate. This would help to prevent politicians from doing a favor for these benefactors. We all could see if for instance a lobby group donated money to a super-Pac and then later if a politician helped with legislation which would benefit this lobby group.

Many times, when someone in Congress receives a large donation, then later they write legislation that will benefit this large donor and slide it into a spending bill at the last moment. Many of these "sliders" are tax loopholes which benefit the large donors. This is the very reason the Tax Code is so large and cumbersome, and continues to grow. A simplified tax structure would help stop this system of self-interests overshadowing the well-being of the greater good.

Redistricting in most states allow state lawmakers to design congressional districts to protect incumbents. Members of both parties collaborate to pack Republicans and Democrats in their own districts to create districts for those then in power. If we look at the facts, over the past ten years, three fourths of congressional districts have never switched party, according to John Fortier, Director of the Democracy Project at the Bipartisan Policy Center. We Americans should prevent politicians from choosing their own voters.

One solution to this: California has a fourteen member Citizens Redistricting Committee composed of five Democrats, five Republicans, and four from neither party. This and all major decisions on redistricting have to have support from all three groups. And this 14 member committee held public hearings and operated transparently! Another possible solution is how Iowan's do it, there non-partisan technocrats redraw congressional lines.

We need leaders who will work for the highest good for all of us and for the good of planet Earth. Right now a self-evident truth is this mostly doesn't happen because many of our politicians are more concerned about getting re-elected or in acquiring more power.

A solution to this is to enact term-limits, such as we have for the President, ratified by the twentieth Amendment of our Constitution. It may not be possible for the current Congress to pass such a law, because many of our Senators and Congressmen wouldn't want to lose their jobs or their power. However we Americans could prevail by electing a Congress who will tackle the issues facing us today or by working through our State Legislators to call for a Constitutional Amendment.

Term limits would help in many ways, one of which would be – people would sign up to be of service for a term or two at most, and realize they are serving the greater good, rather than being self-serving.

Another benefit would be the dollars we would save which are paid out in pensions for these elected officials, because there would not be a need for any pensions. By having dedicated servants for the greater good, it should help relieve much of the gridlock we now see.

Another possibility, do we still need the Electoral College today? With the advent of computer generated voting and almost instant tallying of results, the popular vote should be all we need.

An interesting fact is that about 50% of Americans vote – versus 95% for Australia. In Australia they impose a small fine if their citizens don't vote. This may help show the importance to Americans to get out and vote, because many Americans don't think their vote counts. When more Americans take their right to vote seriously, this may make "the silent majorities" presence known. This could change the political landscape and foster the move to more fairness and unity.

5 THE AMERICANS

Another possible solution to reducing the gridlock and increasing the "work together attitude" would be to have a viable third party along with the Democratic and Republican parties. It seems today, as if many in these two dominant parties are off to the right or off to the left on many issues. This causes difference of opinion which can't seem to be rectified. A party more in the center could help bridge the gaps between us all and offer solutions for the highest good for all. Possibly this party could be called: The Americans!

The American Party would be we who care about our country and about each other. We would be fiscally responsible and have an attitude of service for the greater good. The possible color for this party could be white to go along with red and blue for the other parties. Red, white, and blue! White signifies purity and could represent self-evident solutions and ideals.

A possible mascot could be the Bald Eagle. It is already a proud symbol of Americans. The eagle flies high and can see the big picture clearly, but also has excellent vision and can focus on the details as well. This is what is missing now in our country. Many times we make short term decisions that don't take into account long term consequences. We should think through several different scenarios that would test the decisions of today for a secure tomorrow.

It should be self-evident that a leader should do what is right for the highest good for all of us and then their constituency. This way if someone or some entity supports a candidate, this is a positive way to help change the way things are. It is much better than being opposed to someone. If we support who and what we think creates the highest good, then the rest should take care of itself. This concept also should segue into civility in campaigns and other matters when difference of opinion is at hand.

We Americans while being individuals, are part of the greater whole of humankind, and when we treat others with respect, when we listen and try to understand other points of view, this can facilitate more clear understanding. Even if we still don't agree with someone or some idea, we can allow other people to explain their point of view, and then take our turn explaining ours. There is no need to belittle someone else or their ideas. This is a childish action which may have worked when we were children, but now as adults we should know better and act accordingly.

Campaigns which attempt to tear down an idea or to destroy the integrity of another fellow American is counterproductive and destructive. This leads to the downward spiral of negativity and can create hostility which is a further erosion of the common good. When we are positive in our approach to others and to our ideas, we can lead by example and let the self-evident truth lead to transparency. Being for someone or something is much more beneficial to all concerned compared with being against something or someone.

We all have varying knowledge and experiences so our viewpoint will come from our past knowledge and experience. However we can open our minds to acceptance, tolerance and understanding, while showing respect for all – even when we choose to agree to disagree. Our nation's founding slogan is spot on - *E Pluribus Unum:* out of many, one.

6 FAIRNESS & UNITY

Our free market society works well for the most part, but when unfairness creeps in and creates an ever widening divide between the "haves and the have not's," then it is time for compassionate action. We Americans and our government should be ever watchful for times when our economic system becomes unbalanced and provide solutions for restoring the equilibrium.

Most people do not like change, but it is a fact of life, change is part of living, and those who resist change are not being truthful to themselves. We embrace change by being aware and watchful for opportunities to improve our way of life – for all Americans. Solutions for the greater good is the only way to continue to provide the American dream that our founders set in motion at the start of our United States of America. It is up to us to work together and provide solutions so every American can have the necessities of life, including affordable health care.

The National Football League is an example of an organization which pools its revenues and spreads the money around, so all cities have a chance to create a winning team. There are 32 teams from cities ranging from millions of people, such as New York, to one such as Green Bay. In this manner, the total revenue is divided between the teams in a way which is equitable and fair. It is also interesting that the NFL is very successful, even when it uses money that the large city teams brought in and funnels it to the smaller city teams. This is the concept of sharing the wealth by helping those in need, for the greater good.

We need to examine the inflow of revenue and the outflow of expenses and make changes so the important values of our society are reflected in everyday life. We shouldn't think that we should get something for nothing, because we all have a stake in this great nation, and so sacrifice or conscious supportive action is the way to secure our rights. When we move away from the concept of me and mine, we move to the compassionate way of living where we share in the bounty which is all around us. We Americans will continue on our journey together and provide equitable solutions to solve the injustices and unfairness that many experience each and every day.

7 FINANCIAL SECURITY

Today America's debt is a whopping 14.5 trillion dollars – and still growing!

The current global financial crisis – what is happening now - is what we might call the 'haves' being forced to give some of what they have to the 'have-nots' who have less. If many of us had lived more within our means and given some of what we had to others, willingly, possibly none of this would have happened in the first place.

Deficit spending is another self-evident truth which defies all economic logic. We Americans should know if we spend more than our income, we are heading down the road to personal bankruptcy. The same is true of our great nation: we are heading down the road to financial disaster. Many see this but some throw up their hands and don't see any way out. It really is pretty simple, but of course with any action, there are consequences.

In economics 101, there are three ways to maintain a positive account balance: increase income, reduce expenses, and a combination of the first two. This shouldn't be hard to figure. So why then is Congress arguing about how to fix our soaring debt? It is obvious – we need to utilize the third option of reducing spending and increasing income – Now! Our country is deep in debt yet our government is avoiding its budget cutting responsibilities.

Federal Reserve Chairman, Ben Bernanke says we are facing a real "fiscal cliff," and it is coming unless we cut the deficit. Yes there will be consequences or sacrifices, but to do nothing and kick the can down the road for future Americans to deal with is not a viable option. This is because soon we will reach the "tipping point" and then it will be too late. None of us want to go there, and now is the time to put our heads together and solve this financial crisis. Today our tax revenue as a percentage of our Gross Domestic Product has to returned to levels similar to what we had in the 50's.

We need to increase revenue by raising taxes on the wealthy, do away with the plethora of the tax incentives we dole out to many corporations, and of course reduce the expenditures of the government. How do we accomplish this? By level-headed discussions and providing solutions that are based on truthful statistics. For example: how many government agencies do we really need? Is bigger government better? Well our founding fathers argued about this too, but the basic reason for a federal government was to maintain our security against threats from abroad.

Today we have so many laws and regulations that it is difficult to determine which ones we truly need and which ones should be eliminated. Why do we need so many attorneys? In our recent past, Americans didn't rush out to sue a neighbor; we worked through most of our differences. We also had doctors who served our needs and charged a fair and affordable fee. What happened? The meme (idea or group of ideas that replicate and spread) of me and mine rears its ugly head again!

We must reign in spending too, in a fair and equitable way, but not leave Americans in the lurch to make ends meet. There are many solutions of how to do this, and some may seem more painful than others, but a combination of many of them is the order of the day.

Medicare and Medicaid continue to gobble up a greater portion of the American budget and will continue unless we figure this out. We could investigate how to reduce or stop fraud for one thing. Means testing would also help here, because if someone has lots of money, should our government provide benefits which could go to those who really need them? If we provided more preventative procedures, we would reduce the costs of escalating disease before they occurred. It is self-evident that it is our choice to smoke or not, and the facts clearly show that smoking causes many costly health related problems. Possibly we could levy higher taxes on tobacco products and funnel those new tax dollars to pay for tobacco related illnesses and treatment.

In the state of Utah, private insurance companies have a medical surcharge for smokers on Medicaid. They are also considering higher co-payments for tobacco users. They cite the facts from the American Lung Association: smokers enrolled in Medicaid smoke at a rate 60% greater than the general population. The increase of the co-pay by two to three dollars or the possibility of paying more for their insurance may help. And these proposals include a wellness aspect including a smoking cessation program. These insurers are also debating whether to extend these ideas to include obesity and alcohol abuse. In Denmark, they have a "fat tax," which levies high taxes on high fat foods, and obesity in Denmark is not a major issue.

The financial security of older Americans is a basic tenant of the pursuit of happiness. However Social Security continues to comprise more of the American budget. When Social Security was fist enacted, it was basically to help the elderly who had no family or means to support themselves during the Depression. The retirement age was 65 and many Americans lived only a few years after retirement. Also, many elderly Americans were taken in by their families in years gone by and this may be part of the solution now. Many of us are living in larger homes than previous generations, which could provide a living space for a parent or a relative. Today more and more Americans are retiring early and living much longer. Possibly means testing here would also help solve some of the funding dilemma. Those with considerable wealth don't need Social Security benefits. It also may be necessary to raise the retirement age to 67 and eliminate early retirement.

Another anomaly in the equation is what many call "double dipping." This is when someone retires with a pension from some corporation or government job, and then collects Social Security too. It should be obvious, that this is not fair and keeps dollars from those who really need help. Another way for someone to "double dip" is when a government employee or another retired pensioner retires and receives their pension, and then returns to the workforce and earns a substantial living – on top of their pension. Some even earn wages commensurate with what they earned just before they retired. This knocks out younger Americans looking for work and their pay would be much less than what the "retired double-dipper" is making.

Is it possible for a group of professional business people to look for ways to streamline our government agencies and the processes they use today? Sure it is. Successful business owners do this regularly and adjust their business model to meet the changing demands of the marketplace. However in government, laws are passed creating agencies or increasing funding for one already established, but rarely are we Americans involved in rationally discerning which agencies or departments are in need of reduction or elimination. So our government grows with each passage of a bill creating yet another agency and adds to the behemoth of governmental bureaucracy. It is time to take stock of what we have and make the necessary decisions to streamline our government so it is really "for the people."

Our government was meant to be small and to be of service to us. What has happened is it has grown gigantic and is devouring our hard earned dollars and we are going in debt to fund the system which was initially devised to serve and protect. It is self-evident our governments are mired in their own bureaucracy which continues to grow beyond that which they were created for. It will take much hard work and tough decisions on how to wrestle this giant back into submission to serve and protect.

A solution which could work right now, is to require all departments and agencies to systematically prepare a budget which includes an across the board 10% reduction. Some businesses do this on a regular basis, or when it is needed because of lower sales etc. It is obvious our government is living beyond its means, so we need to trim the fat and raise revenues. It is almost inconceivable to borrow money to run the government, but it has become the norm. Today America's debt is a whopping 14.5 trillion dollars – and still growing! This must stop and we must insist on bringing down the debt by reducing deficit spending. Our goal should be first to become debt free and then run a balanced budget from there on out. This would create a much stronger America for us and for our posterity.

It is evident that many countries including ours are not building a secure future, but deluding ourselves to spend now and worry later. Later is now, and if we don't act together to figure this mess out, there will be chaos and hard times soon. Why? Because our past wasteful decisions and actions are rising up to create many situations which could bring us to our knees. Some examples are: dependence on foreign oil – or oil in general, borrowing money to pay for excess, being the world's policeman, sheltering the wealthy at the expense of those who struggle to survive, etc. We Americans are a blend of many faiths, nationalities, creeds, races – and this is what gives us strength and fortitude. It also can cause us to splinter off into groups of those like us, and try for advantages over others. What is needed though is to look at each other with compassion and search for our similarities to work through our differences by finding common ground.

Have you ever noticed a governmental agency that says it has too much money and decides to cut its own budget? Some of this has to do with retaining and gaining power. Many of our departments or agencies run themselves and don't want to share information or best practices. We should insist this should stop.

8 OMBUDSMANSHIP

Webster's Collegiate Dictionary - eleventh edition, defines an ombudsman as: "one that investigates reported complaints (as from students or consumers), reports findings, and helps to achieve equitable settlements." Across the globe, people are protesting and asking for change, but the outcome so far is bloodshed and/or regime change. It is possible to set up a governmental department or a committee where people can bring issues or recommendations for improvement. These ideas can then be put to the test of fact finding to see if these ideas have merit. If so, then this committee could act as liaison to other departments and to the governmental leader such as the mayor, governor, or President.

This committee could be chaired by an elected official or an appointed one. Members could be lay people volunteering their service and/or government employees.

Countries such as Sweden and New Zealand have established ombudsmanship to help bring the government closer to the people. This would provide a service that is of the people and for the people. Innovation and ideas could flow from Americans and be heard. Imagination is the core of our strength and when we imagine a better way to do something, or to bring equality into the very center of what we do, we build on a strong foundation which we can continue to build this great nation.

9 CORPORATIONS

During the 1880's, a new entity was born – the corporation. These corporations were empowered and given the same rights as us Americans, but without a moral conscience or an eye for the good of all of us. Many corporations exist for one reason, to make a profit, and sometimes at any cost. Our ancestors allowed the creation of a purely materialistic, mechanical, and nonliving entity. Laws were passed allowing corporations power over humanity. In days past, The Golden Rule, where we did unto others as we would have done to us, was replaced by the Rule of Gold – or materialism.

The rise of big stateless corporations, many of which rival many countries in terms of political and economic power, have caused some of the inequality in our world. Globalization has also shielded these huge corporations and helped them achieve more attractive tax shelters and less regulatory control. The first corporations were created to serve the countries in which they were founded. However through the years, these large companies took advantage of their elevated status – which allowed them to grow exponentially and shape political landscapes.

From here, these corporations, many of which are monopolies, have helped create laws which swung the balance of power to their advantage. These corporations have evolved from the legal entities created to ensure a company would survive the death of its owners, to today having more rights than we Americans do. The biggest companies have the economic and political influence similar to all countries but the largest thirty or so. These borderless global corporations have changed the international order; however the rules and ways to govern them haven't changed. The ideas which gave national governments their authority have been diminished.

Today we hear about the way in which larger governments curtail rather than protect and improve individual freedoms. This is similar to what occurred and caused the English, French and American Revolutions.

Why should we allow corporations supremacy over us Americans? Why should we allow American corporations to incorporate in other countries for tax benefits or to send their money to tax shelters in other countries?

Corporations are run by the CEO who reports to the board of directors. Many of the board members are employees of the corporation or friends of the officers. This way many of the people charged with oversight of the CEO and company practices, have vested interests in their own compensation and of course the stock price. In many of the corporations, there is little time spent on how the corporation affects our society as a whole. Is it a good citizen or not. If we find a politician who does not have the good of all at heart, then we can choose to elect someone else in the future. But what can we do about a corporation which chooses to trample on the rights of Americans?

Can we reign in the rights of corporations and ensure oversight of these boards of directors? It is possible and should be investigated.

10 HEALTH CARE

We Americans should all be entitled to affordable health care, however many Americans do not have health insurance. The United States is the only major economy where millions of Americans are not covered by health insurance, mainly because it is not affordable. Are we not a society who cares about our fellow Americans?

To answer the why to this predicament, we must look at the powers to be who wish to keep the "status quo" as it is because many benefit financially by resisting the inevitable change which is coming. Many pharmaceutical companies, insurance companies, hospitals, and medical professionals don't want to affect their own profit and income.

If more of us were satisfied with earning a respectable wage and helping those less fortunate at the same time, we would have health coverage for every American. Most of America's allies already have a health care system which enables all of its citizens to have access to health care. Our closest neighbor, Canada, has a successful health care system and their economy is nowhere near the size of ours. For example an angiogram in Canada costs $35 compared to $798 here in America. Another example is a MRI in France costs $281 but here it costs $1080.

Some other countries have more affordable health care such as Switzerland, France, and Taiwan. Twenty years ago Switzerland was at a place similar to ours today, and they decided to cause all of its people to purchase private health care and in this way it made health care more affordable for all of its citizens. Today every Swiss citizen has access to health care and the costs have moderated. The Swiss spend 11% of its Gross Domestic Product on health care, however here in America we spend 17% of our GDP – the most by far of any other industrialized country. Also the Swiss citizens are not tied to their employers for health care but can choose among many available plans.

Taiwan decided in the 90's to choose a new health care system which provided universal coverage but went with one provider – similar to our Medicare – but for all citizens. Today Taiwan spends 7% of its GDP! No other nation spends more than 12% of its GDP – except us Americans at 17% and climbing.

Another fact is that American companies pay billions of dollars for the health care of its employees and retired employees. However in England, Germany, Canada, and Japan, their corporations don't have to pay much in comparison to American companies. This hinders American corporations against our global competitors. Other nations such as those listed above provide health care for all of their citizens at much lower costs than we do and have better results such as higher life expectancy, lower obesity and diabetes, and lower infant mortality. Interestingly the citizens of these other countries are more satisfied with their health care than many Americans.

It is a fact that prescription drugs cost much more in America than they do in other countries. Why? Shouldn't the drugs be the same price – regardless of where a specific drug is purchased?

The medical profession in America primarily deals with prescribing drugs to counter symptoms, such as taking a pain medication to alleviate pain, or swallowing a pill to lower cholesterol. What about determining the cause of the pain or the high cholesterol and then working on a regimen to healing? Many Americans would rather take the easy way and swallow the pill than try new ways to reduce stress, exercise, or adjust their diet to reduce cholesterol.

Alternative medicine is not new however many American physicians don't believe that alternatives will work, because they were not taught about alternatives in medical school. Many of the Eastern medical solutions deal with prevention and healing. It is important to understand the energy flows of our bodies and then work towards releasing our blocked energy, which can cause many ailments. Alternative medicine is a holistic way to treat and cure "issues in the tissues," rather than covering up the symptoms. We should support Alternative Medicine Practitioners, rather than trying to staunch these healing ways. More emphasis on prevention is needed and would reduce health care costs dramatically.

Doctors who care and give discounts to those of more limited means would help the less fortunate as opposed to those doctors who don't. An example: one instance an insurance company discounted several procedures so the patient paid about half of what was originally billed. However the next time these same procedures were conducted, the insurance company did not discount the procedures and the doctor wanted full payment for the procedures. The first time the doctor accepted the reduced amount but not the second time. The patient was expected to pay the full amount – even though the patient was on limited fixed income and asked for assistance. What we find today in America is some insurance companies cancelling insurance coverage and/or denying coverage for pre-existing conditions. This is not fair or unitive in action.

Millions of our fellow Americans are left out and feel unwanted and so the American dream of the pursuit of happiness is not really for them, because of health issues or even medical bankruptcy. If we are truly a compassionate society, this would not be. We have the power to insist on change so we All can share in the abundance our great land affords.

11 INCARCERATION

Many of us understand that our penal system is broken and needs major adjustments. The prison population continues to rise dramatically and so do the costs associated with maintaining those incarcerated. Today we have more than six million inmates in prison – more than even Stalin had under his notorious regime. America has 760 prisoners per 100,000 of population! The country with the next highest is Brazil with 242 per 100,000. Other countries per 100,000 of population: Mexico – 208, England – 153, S. Korea – 97, and Japan – 63.

Americans make up five percent of the world's population but we have 25% of the world's prisoners. New prisons are being built of which the costs are staggering. It is obvious that what we are now doing – isn't working. During 2011 California spent 9.6 billion on its prison system versus the 5.7 billion it spent for the universities and state colleges. A college student in California costs the state $8,667 per year, while a prisoner costs $45,006 per year!

The big gap between America and the other nations has ballooned since the early eighties. In 1980 we had 150 prisoners per 100,000 of population. It has multiplied more than four times since then. Why? Incarceration from drug convictions has gone from 15 per 100,000 to 148 in 1996. More than half of the inmates today are there because of drug convictions, and 4 out of 5 of these convictions are for possession. Possibly the legalization of marijuana would help here. In this way we can cut into the drug cartels profit and tax the use of marijuana to create more revenue. A group of 300 economists - who call themselves, "Endorsing Economists," say America could save 7.7 billion dollars a year, by not enforcing the laws concerning marijuana possession. They also say if we taxed marijuana like tobacco, we could raise another 6 billion in revenue.

We may also want to scrutinize the privatization of our prisons. Many state prisons are run by private companies which have lobbyists in our state capitols. Hmm, follow the money trail. The money America spends on prisons has gone up six times the rate of expenses for higher education.

Another solution is to make time in prison much tougher on those inside, so it would be a greater deterrent to make more would-be inmates think again about going to prison. First of all, we could establish that every inmate would perform some type of work, without pay, and this work would help reduce the costs of running the prison. Farming, laundry, gardening, sewing, cleaning, painting, manufacturing, printing, landscaping, are some of many.

Rehabilitation is another method to work with those inside and help them realize it is their choices which got them in trouble in the first place. When we understand first there are other choices and when we choose the higher choices, then we can begin to see a broader selection of possibilities. Learning a trade, learning how to be more productive on the outside can also help.

The focus should be on helping those who desire help, and to be tougher on those who decide they don't want help or refuse the participatory part of their incarceration.

Of course when we provide the opportunity for all Americans to have the basics needs of life, and when we narrow the gap between the wealthy and the rest of us, and create more jobs, this will create more of an atmosphere of equality and compassion. This would reduce the number of people who would choose to take away from the greater good. Instead we would have Americans who choose to add substance to our communities and be helpful participants in building our bright future.

12 IMMIGRATION

We Americans welcome those who want to come to America – those who immigrate legally. Today we have many who seek to circumvent the legal process to become American citizens. It should be self-evident, that the benefits of living in America are what draws millions of people who desire freedom and opportunity. Also, if we allow these non-citizens many of the benefits we all enjoy – without going through the legal process of applying for permission to relocate here, then this exacerbates the problem.

Anyone who uses stealth and subversion to come in under the radar of our legal system should not be allowed to work in America or receive any of the benefits bestowed on legal applicants. This in itself would stem much of the flow of illegal immigrants into our nation.

Building walls and policing the borders will not curb this flow. Abiding by the laws of the land will do this, if we fairly apply them in all situations. Fraudulent use of fake identification should not be tolerated. We should institute a fool-proof process of identifying false documents and require businesses to verify this documentation. Penalties to those who hire illegal immigrants should be increased and enforced. For those who choose to come to America illegally, we should make the reasons to come here illegally, not worth it.

English is the language of Americans, and so all people who desire to become citizens here, should learn the English language. This should be a provision in becoming an American citizen and could also be another hurdle that many may choose not to jump and thus stay in their own country until they learn English.

Theodore Roosevelt declared in 1907: "In the first place, we should insist that if the immigrant who comes here in good faith becomes an American and assimilates himself to us, he shall be treated on an exact equality with everyone else, for it is an outrage to discriminate against any such man because of creed, or birthplace, or origin. But this is predicated upon the person's becoming in every facet an American, and nothing but an American . . . There can be no divided allegiance here. Any man who says he is an American, but something else also, isn't an American at all. We have room for but one flag, the American flag . . . We have room for but one language here, and that is the English language . . . And we have room for but one sole loyalty and that loyalty is to the American People."

We are one nation built on the idea that any person from any country can come to America to pursue the "American Dream." And these people need to follow the due process and rules already in force.

13 EDUCATION

Our system of education is lacking in many areas and especially when compared to other industrialized nations. When we seriously observe what is happening, it is obvious what we are now doing is not serving us Americans well. Teaching knowledge is one thing, but teaching subjects like: critical thinking, personal finance, participatory action, solution analysis, listening, speaking, how to raise children, how to have a successful marriage, etc. can provide the necessary catalyst to help our children learn life skills which will serve them well now and in the future.

For this to occur, parents, teachers, and leaders, need to show by example, the American way. For instance, learning respect for other people is crucial for our nation to evolve upward in a civil society. Children need to learn accepted boundaries and routines, at home, at school, at church, and in all aspects of our society. This includes learning discipline and consequences when someone steps outside these boundaries. An example would be to learn the benefits of being punctual and the detriment of not being punctual. Every action creates a consequence, and when the consequence is seen to be negative, most people will try to avoid behavior which does not give them the positive benefit.

Some cultures in the past utilized the wise elders of the community to teach their children. In this way, those who have learned through life lessons can relay their experiences through anecdote and speak from what they have learned. Where do new parents today learn how to parent? Through trial and error. Why not teach the pros and cons of ways to parent before one becomes a parent? Topics such as ways to discipline, setting boundaries, commitment, could be put to good use by all young Americans.

John Wellwood wrote: "The role of an effective teacher is to instruct, encourage and correct the student, as well as to provide an example of what is possible. Effective teachers also try to see what individual students most need at each step of their development, rather than trying to fit the student into a pre-programmed agenda . . . A step toward recognizing their own authority – that they are indeed authors of their own experience, rather than passive victims of circumstance. The acid test is not how well the student pleases the teacher, but how fully they meet and respond to life's challenges."

Where do our children learn to think for themselves? We should add to our curriculum the topic of critical thinking, where we teach them to think on their own. Perhaps we could develop typical scenarios and then allow the students through discussions to arrive at a mutually agreeable solution. To do this effectively, we could teach the benefits of first open-thinking, where any and all ideas are welcome. Then we start closed-thinking where we analyze the details and then make decisions based on the facts.

When trying to find an equitable solution, there are several steps necessary to arriving at one agreeable to most. Looking at the situation and analyzing the facts can help to provide a framework for the ultimate solution. This first step is crucial to ensure we are working on the right problem. Obtaining agreement from others is vital. Next is determining what is causing this problem in the first place. Every situation or problem is caused by something or many things, and this provides a way to systematically search for the underlying cause. Thirdly is the open forum of deciding how to solve the problem and again any and all ideas are accepted and acknowledged. When this list of possibilities is exhausted, then it is necessary to narrow the field down to one or a few solutions – which then becomes the best solution attainable.

Of course once we have a solution, it is necessary to implement it so an analysis of how to implement this solution is tantamount to successful resolution. Here the need to consider implementation steps in logical order of completion and who to communicate to are critical. Of course, the solution may change depending on the make-up of the group of individuals engaged in this process of critical thinking. We must be aware that no one person has the "right" answer and we may find better answers together. If our first attempt does not succeed, we can return to our list of possible solutions and try another.

Coming around full circle, parents need to follow these steps in their own lives and provide an open forum for decision making that includes all family members. Many times, children have ideas which will work, if we only listen and facilitate their involvement.

14 FOREIGN POLICY

When we lead by example, this is the strongest method to influence others. Saying one thing and then doing another is most times seen as a ruse and is not what leadership encompasses. Is it our prerogative to preach the American way, or to live it?

When we have our own house in order, it is much easier to show how we Americans are benefiting from our democratic society. It is not necessary to try and push "our way" on others. Our actions speak much louder than our words so let our democracy and our freedom lead by example, in this way other countries may want the benefits we enjoy.

We cannot and should not be the policeman of the world. We should of course have a strong military as a defense against anyone trying to subvert our precious society. Also when our allies request our help in aiding another country in need, our strength and compassion would prevail. This strength and unwavering loyalty to the important tenants of our society, is what our forefathers wanted in our federal government. Protect and defend.

Providing aid to other countries should be limited and serious oversight into the use of that precious aid is necessary. Our resources are limited and we should choose wisely when and where we will allocate our hard earned capital.

Going to war should always be a last resort. Certainly when America is threatened then this is a time to use our military to defend our liberty. A fact we sometimes neglect to see is that our military budget is by far the largest in the world. This is one of the reasons other countries are prospering now, because they use their money to strengthen their own economy and add jobs, instead of spending huge sums on a standing military.

Our country is enmeshed in what is called, "the military industrial complex," where our defense department has very close ties to large defense contractors. War is big business for some of these corporations. We must be aware and vigilant so that we Americans don't go to war without the consent of the governed, and send our sons and daughters to fight without a true mission to accomplish.

When we examine Americans involvement in wars over our history, most wars, until recent times, were to protect democracy and defend our country from other countries. The war in Korea and Viet Nam changed how America uses its military might. Instead of fighting to preserve our freedom, we tried to stop another country from invading another nation – without the mission to win.

More recently the decision to invade Iraq to find the supposed weapons of mass destruction was made without gaining approval of our allies. And then when we found no such weapons, we didn't return our son's and daughter's home. As we have found, it is next to impossible to occupy a country and accomplish any mission because many of the people of that occupied country despise the occupiers.

We should have looked at the failures to occupy Afghanistan by other countries in the past and realized it is not feasible to occupy this country and stabilize it. This is because of the disunity of the many varied factions and issues within Afghanistan. The mission there cannot be attained so we should exit Afghanistan now.

Our president should receive approval from congress before declaring war or sending our precious sons & daughters to fight overseas. Also attaining support from our allies is important as well. By building a strong America, this will show other nations by our example, how our freedom and democracy benefit all Americans. Many other nations will want to follow our lead, and try for reform of their own countries, instead of America trying to reform them.

America spends 600 billion dollars each year on our military and we could certainly use some of our hard earned dollars to support America's priorities at home.

One glaring issue that plagues us here in America is the oversight when spending public monies. Many of us have heard of the proverbial "hundred dollar hammer" or the "five hundred dollar toilet seat." Some laugh at this but it is no laughing matter. In the business world, a company could not survive without auditors and others charged to ensuring a strategy is working and we are receiving the best bang for the dollars spent. The same should apply to any government agency. When Congress establishes an agency or a solution to a problem, included in this should be the means to review and ensure our targets are hit.

Bi-partisan committees, which could include business men and women, should be established for oversight and be responsible for being the watch-dogs of where taxpayer money is spent. It may seem at first to add to the governmental bureaucracy we have today, but it is necessary to wisely monitor what we intend and to ensure we achieve our goals. If not, then this agency or this process should be re-worked or eliminated.

15 WELFARE & UNEMPLOYMENT BENEFITS

The current system of providing money and services for those who are down on their luck is broken. The fact that we have families who, generations after generation are on the governmental dole should not happen. When we make things too easy for our citizens to "quit and stay," receiving money when they are entirely capable to provide for themselves needs to stop. This fosters the thought that we are owed something from the government without any effort on our part.

Today, 8.1% of Americans are unemployed, but when we factor in those who have been employed longer than one year, the real percentage would really be around 15%. This is because some of these unemployed Americans have decided to stop looking for work. When we keep extending the unemployment benefits, it removes the impetus to actually find gainful employment.

Right now, Spain has 24% unemployment and 50% unemployment for those under 25! And of course they are close to insolvency. We Americans certainly don't want to go there and experience what could soon be chaos.

Another fact is that many companies say they can't find the employees with the proper skills to do the more technical jobs they need today. Many small manufacturers and trucking companies report the lack of skilled workers. Many retail companies can't find enough workers because some Americans don't see those service jobs as good enough for them, so these service positions go unfilled.

A way to improve on this unfortunate situation is to provide a means for those who need temporary help, is to have something similar to the Public Works Program. Here we could provide jobs for those who can't seem to find them in the private sector, and help improve America's infrastructure at the same time. Instead of letting things like bridges, schools, highways, etc. to continue to deteriorate, we could use the hard work of Americans to improve the very heart of our nation.

By putting many able bodied Americans to work productively for our benefit, we move dollars from supporting inactivity to building a stronger America. This would shift money from welfare to building a strong infrastructure.

There should be time-limits on welfare and unemployment funds for each individual and the focus should be on getting off these programs and becoming a viable part of our economic strength. Certainly we all may need some help from time to time, and again why shouldn't families be more involved in providing a helping hand? It seems that many Americans want independence but we are all inter-dependent, so let's look for solutions which move us towards our values such as compassion and opportunity.

16 ENVIRONMENTAL STEWARDSHIP

It is self-evident that the Earth is in need of our commitment, to ensure we save our natural environment from the brink of destruction and no return. We are now drilling, digging, deforesting, paving, burning, combusting, and mining, towards the tipping point where our beautiful Earth will not be able to recover. Our need for stored ancient sunlight such as coal, oil, and natural gas is creating a whole in the earth and in our ozone layer which protects us from harmful radiation. Greenhouse gasses exacerbate the problem by keeping in more of the heat and raising the temperature of the earth. Pollution is killing many species around the world and our water supply is contaminated with many lethal toxins. Some Americans will doubt these facts, but they are facts indeed.

The practice of drilling deep into the earth to dispose of human waste and the by-products of fracking, should not be tolerated. Some say this is not harmful to the earth but eventually these toxins will leach into our precious fresh water supply. Certainly there are ways to detoxify waste products and reuse them, instead of pumping and dumping hazardous materials into and onto the earth.

It would be wise to discuss best practices from around the world to help solve our problems through ecology, recycling, and stewardship. It is in all of our best interest for this to occur and to secure the future of our beautiful planet for our children, grandchildren and beyond.

There are good ideas already in place in different countries or areas of the world, and it seems we here in America are behind on some of them. An example is the way we heat our hot water. Many countries in Europe use tankless water heaters at the point of use. Instead of heating water and storing it in a large hot water tank, the tankless heater heats only what is necessary. This eliminates constantly heating the water in the tank and also the water in the myriad of pipes till hot water reaches its destination. It also eliminates the waste of heated water sitting in the pipes after the use is finished, thus saving energy.

Today, most of our energy in America comes from fossil fuels such as coal, oil, and natural gas. These fuels are limited and obtaining these fuels scars the earth in many ways. The use of renewable sources of energy is what we need to convert to – and soon. There are many proven ways to do this, but here in America, we lag or drag our feet. Why? Many times it is as simple as following the money trail. Who benefits from continuing our dependency on fossil fuels?

Some of the renewable sources of energy are: solar, wind, wave, and hydrogen cells. All of them should be the major focus for America's future energy needs. Collecting the suns energy in solar panels and converting it into electricity is simple and the costs continue to come down, but we here in

America are way behind other countries in implementing and adding solar energy to our electric grids. The sun provides 50,000 times as much energy as we need all over the world. All countries should tap into this plentiful and renewable source – and the sooner the better! One possible solution would be to emphasize the need for all new construction to include solar panels to produce energy for the buildings and to add any excess to the grid. Another solution would be to provide incentives to add solar panels to existing homes and commercial buildings now.

Hydrogen cells take the most plentiful resource on earth – water – and extract hydrogen which we can burn without pollution, because what is left over from extracting hydrogen from water is oxygen!

Recycling should also be the norm, and not the exception. We Americans throw out way too much junk that ends up in landfills, which eventually harms the environment by leaching toxic materials into the ground water and beyond. Possibly we could enact penalties for those who do not recycle and use those funds to further ecological pursuits.

The availability of clean fresh water continues to be harder to come by and there are methods to help recycle water as well.

For instance, rain barrels or cisterns to collect rain water could be one way to help save water. This collected water could be used for irrigation, and other uses where potable water is not necessary. Another idea which is not used much but could especially help in the warmer climates is to collect the condensation from air conditioners, refrigerators, etc. Much of this precious water seeps into the ground without much help for plants etc. or is dumped into the sewers. Reclaiming this clean water could be used to water house plants, outdoor plants, gardens, etc.

A solution to help in this area is the idea of a "Watering Bucket" which could collect this condensate and using it for watering plants and gardens. It could consist of a gallon size bucket with a lid. Two holes would be drilled into the top, one for a spout to be added and the other for a funnel to be inserted into. This watering bucket would then be placed under the dripping air conditioner or other condensate device and collect this precious clean water. From there it can be used to nourish our plants. It is also possible to set up multiple storage buckets to collect even more condensate, similar to methods already in use to collect rain from downspouts.

Our focus must change from the "use and throw away," mentality to the "use wisely and recycle," concept. More bulk packaging instead of single-use packaging would help. Also ensuring the packaging is biodegradable would prevent packaging to sit forever in landfills. In this way, we all become stewards of our planet and change the way we look at "Mother Earth." She provides all we need but we are taking more than we need and doing it in many ways where we are past the point of no return. If we don't realize and stop the deforestation of our planet, soon we will not have enough trees to provide the necessary oxygen for us to breathe. The trees take carbon dioxide, which is a major source of greenhouse gases, through photosynthesis and the suns power produces sugar and oxygen.

We are cutting down forests to provide wood, paper, and ground for mining and raising beef cattle. One way which would help save many trees is farming the hemp plant, which is easy to grow without much pesticide or fertilizer, to provide many uses such as paper, clothing, and rope. Utilizing hemp is more cost effective to farm than trees, and so we could leave much of the tree-farms revert back to old-growth forests which help clean our precious air and provide homes for the animals.

We should move towards no-till farming to save the run-off of precious topsoil and to lessen the need for pesticides and herbicides. Of course the use of no-till farming would also lower the need for diesel fuel. The move towards more organic farming would be of great help here too. Through organic farming and the limited use of Genetically Modified food, this would help reduce our overall health care costs.

17 FINAL THOUGHTS

We have covered a myriad of topics and proposed possible solutions – many of which are self-evident. What we need today is for all of us to be more tolerant of each other and work for unity of purpose – which is to support the ideals put forth by our founding fathers: to provide all Americans our "inalienable rights of life, liberty, and the pursuit of happiness." When our focus is on these ideals, we will re-establish our nation as a beacon of freedom where we Americans stand united in purpose to enjoy the fruits of our labor and share in the abundance we all are entitled to.

We should elect leaders who will work for us and for these ideals, and vote out those who try and gain more for themselves or who refuse to negotiate and be part of the solution to a prosperous and happy America.

I believe we are the only country in the world which can lead the way for a new world order. And this would be all of us working together to solve the world's issues through listening, compassion, and cooperation. When we stop fighting and arguing – we can utilize this energy to create win-win solutions to increase the pursuit of happiness all around our wonderful planet. It is possible for us all to experience peace, and happiness, if we desire it, and then through unity, do what it takes to achieve that which we desire.

When we see each of us as equals, there is no one who is superior or inferior. This does not mean we are all the same, because each of us is unique – at the same time – equal in God's perspective. It shouldn't matter what our station is in life, or what our heritage is. Neither should our economic status, the color of our skin, the way we dress, or what sex we are. We should all have equal opportunities to have the basic necessities of life so we can be whatever we choose. We are all precious and equal!

When we join hands and look for ways to improve the subsistence level of all people, this is unitive and inclusive. When more and more people don't have to worry about where their next meal is coming from, or don't have to live in fear for their lives, then they will be able to pursue happiness.

Each act of kindness extended toward another will elevate us all. As more and more of us pay this kindness forward, it is similar to the small snowball at the top of the hill which starts to increase in size as it makes its way down. It expands with all of the kindness, love, and compassion we share. In this way, each of us has the power to make these significant changes in our behavior – which will help create an even more wonderful world to experience. It is what we become that makes the difference, and the choice is ours!

Are we part of the problem or part of the solution? There is no middle ground here. We either are keeping the troubling situations around us or helping alleviate the situation by being and doing something positive and helpful.

When we think about all the labels people use to categorize people – such as: Christian, German, Southerner, radical, liberal, patriot, heretic, etc. – these certainly can separate us instead of unite us. If we choose to be unitive and inclusive, we look at each other as equals and as our friends.

"We can let go of impulses to judge others. We can refuse to feel good about the mistakes or suffering of anyone. We can live the lessons of kindness rather than only read or hear about them in church. We can remove our desire for revenge and replace it with kindness." – Wayne W. Dyer from his book *Wisdom of the Ages.*

With this vision of equality, coupled with and understanding of the distinctive character and value of all beings, we demonstrate higher choices and actions and our service for the whole, and we are devoted to universal well-being.

When we move from gathering things to sharing what we have, from thinking of things as mine to realizing they are really for all of us, then we change these old memes and create positive new ones where our spirits will soar in a unitive approach to life. When we become unitive versus separative, positive versus negative, sharing versus gathering, giving versus taking, loving versus hating, living joyfully versus living miserably, free will versus victim-mentality, grateful versus condemnation - we realize the dream of our founding fathers who wrote: E Pluribus Unum – Out of many - One!

ABOUT THE AUTHOR

The author has a Bachelor of Science in Education from the University of Missouri and he has been a seminar leader helping others to achieve their goals. He owned and ran two businesses and was a member of a regional executive team for a major corporation.

Other books by the author:

My Journey of Self – Awareness - 2007

The Master Key System - 2007

In Step With Life - 2009

A Unitive Spirituality - 2009